BECOMING JOURNAL

Awakening To Your Intuition

ALEXI K. HARTWELL

BALBOA PRESS

A DIVISION OF HAY HOUSE

Balboa Press books may be ordered through booksellers or by contacting:

Balboa Press
A Division of Hay House
1663 Liberty Drive
Bloomington, IN 47403
www.balboapress.com
1 (877) 407-4847

ISBN: 978-1-9822-3519-2 (sc)
ISBN: 978-1-9822-3518-5 (e)

Print information available on the last page.

Balboa Press rev. date: 09/19/2019

BECOMING JOURNAL

You have all the power and answers of the Universe within you. Open up and listen to your inner voice.

Date: _____

Time(s) or Repeating Numbers: _____

Songs: _____

Bible Passages/Books/Other Resources: _____

Animals/Birds: _____

Divination Tools/Crystals: _____

Thoughts/Feelings/Dreams: _____

_____

_____

_____

_____

_____

_____

_____

_____

_____

_____

_____

BECOMING JOURNAL

*Trust that all your life experiences have brought you
to this momentous change. They are propelling you
forward to be the person you were meant to be.*

Date: _____

Time(s) or Repeating Numbers: _____

Songs: _____

Bible Passages/Books/Other Resources: _____

Animals/Birds: _____

Divination Tools/Crystals: _____

Thoughts/Feelings/Dreams: _____

_____

_____

_____

_____

_____

_____

_____

_____

_____

_____

_____

BECOMING JOURNAL

Taking care of your needs is the truest and best form of self-care there is.

Date: _____

Time(s) or Repeating Numbers: _____

Songs: _____

Bible Passages/Books/Other Resources: _____

Animals/Birds: _____

Divination Tools/Crystals: _____

Thoughts/Feelings/Dreams: _____

_____

_____

_____

_____

_____

_____

_____

_____

_____

_____

_____

_____

_____

BECOMING JOURNAL

Release thoughts of the past that are holding you hostage. They no longer have any relevance to today and this moment in time.

Date: _____

Time(s) or Repeating Numbers: _____

Songs: _____

Bible Passages/Books/Other Resources: _____

Animals/Birds: _____

Divination Tools/Crystals: _____

Thoughts/Feelings/Dreams: _____

_____

_____

_____

_____

_____

_____

_____

_____

_____

_____

_____

BECOMING JOURNAL

We create our realities by focusing on thoughts or memories. Find the joy in the moment.

Date: _____

Time(s) or Repeating Numbers: _____

Songs: _____

Bible Passages/Books/Other Resources: _____

Animals/Birds: _____

Divination Tools/Crystals: _____

Thoughts/Feelings/Dreams: _____

_____

_____

_____

_____

_____

_____

_____

_____

_____

_____

_____

BECOMING JOURNAL

You are a beacon of hope for others by being your authentic self.

Date: _____

Time(s) or Repeating Numbers: _____

Songs: _____

Bible Passages/Books/Other Resources: _____

Animals/Birds: _____

Divination Tools/Crystals: _____

Thoughts/Feelings/Dreams: _____

_____

_____

_____

_____

_____

_____

_____

_____

_____

_____

_____

BECOMING JOURNAL

Each day is a new chapter in your life. How do you choose to create today?

Date: _____

Time(s) or Repeating Numbers: _____

Songs: _____

Bible Passages/Books/Other Resources: _____

Animals/Birds: _____

Divination Tools/Crystals: _____

Thoughts/Feelings/Dreams: _____

_____

_____

_____

_____

_____

_____

_____

_____

_____

_____

_____

_____

BECOMING JOURNAL

Believe in yourself. You are one with the Creator and are given the power to create your reality. Think really good thoughts!

Date: _____

Time(s) or Repeating Numbers: _____

Songs: _____

Bible Passages/Books/Other Resources: _____

Animals/Birds: _____

Divination Tools/Crystals: _____

Thoughts/Feelings/Dreams: _____

_____

_____

_____

_____

_____

_____

_____

_____

_____

_____

_____

_____

BECOMING JOURNAL

Breathe in and let the breath go.

Breathe in and let the breath go.

Breathe in and let the breath go.

Date: _____

Time(s) or Repeating Numbers: _____

Songs: _____

Bible Passages/Books/Other Resources: _____

Animals/Birds: _____

Divination Tools/Crystals: _____

Thoughts/Feelings/Dreams: _____

_____

_____

_____

_____

_____

_____

_____

_____

_____

_____

BECOMING JOURNAL

I am loving and lovable.

I am loving and lovable.

I am loving and lovable.

Date: _____

Time(s) or Repeating Numbers: _____

Songs: _____

Bible Passages/Books/Other Resources: _____

Animals/Birds: _____

Divination Tools/Crystals: _____

Thoughts/Feelings/Dreams: _____

_____

_____

_____

_____

_____

_____

_____

_____

_____

_____

BECOMING JOURNAL

You matter.

The fact of your very existence says that you matter and you are valuable.

Date: _____

Time(s) or Repeating Numbers: _____

Songs: _____

Bible Passages/Books/Other Resources: _____

Animals/Birds: _____

Divination Tools/Crystals: _____

Thoughts/Feelings/Dreams: _____

_____

_____

_____

_____

_____

_____

_____

_____

_____

_____

_____

BECOMING JOURNAL

You are more than the label(s) you attach to yourself.

You are a mystical, magical, powerful being of pure love.

Date: _____

Time(s) or Repeating Numbers: _____

Songs: _____

Bible Passages/Books/Other Resources: _____

Animals/Birds: _____

Divination Tools/Crystals: _____

Thoughts/Feelings/Dreams: _____

_____

_____

_____

_____

_____

_____

_____

_____

_____

_____

_____

BECOMING JOURNAL

Other people's reactions are a reflection of them. Do not give anyone permission to tell you who you should be.

Date: _____

Time(s) or Repeating Numbers: _____

Songs: _____

Bible Passages/Books/Other Resources: _____

Animals/Birds: _____

Divination Tools/Crystals: _____

Thoughts/Feelings/Dreams: _____

_____

_____

_____

_____

_____

_____

_____

_____

_____

_____

_____

_____

BECOMING JOURNAL

You were born to be the truest expression of love.

Date: _____

Time(s) or Repeating Numbers: _____

Songs: _____

Bible Passages/Books/Other Resources: _____

Animals/Birds: _____

Divination Tools/Crystals: _____

Thoughts/Feelings/Dreams: _____

_____

_____

_____

_____

_____

_____

_____

_____

_____

_____

_____

BECOMING JOURNAL

You are exactly where you are supposed to be.

All is in Divine and perfect order.

Date: _____

Time(s) or Repeating Numbers: _____

Songs: _____

Bible Passages/Books/Other Resources: _____

Animals/Birds: _____

Divination Tools/Crystals: _____

Thoughts/Feelings/Dreams: _____

_____

_____

_____

_____

_____

_____

_____

_____

_____

_____

_____

_____

BECOMING JOURNAL

Find joy in every activity that you do.

Date: _____

Time(s) or Repeating Numbers: _____

Songs: _____

Bible Passages/Books/Other Resources: _____

Animals/Birds: _____

Divination Tools/Crystals: _____

Thoughts/Feelings/Dreams: _____

_____

_____

_____

_____

_____

_____

_____

_____

_____

_____

_____

_____

BECOMING JOURNAL

Honor and value your own needs and desires first.

Date: _____

Time(s) or Repeating Numbers: _____

Songs: _____

Bible Passages/Books/Other Resources: _____

Animals/Birds: _____

Divination Tools/Crystals: _____

Thoughts/Feelings/Dreams: _____

_____

_____

_____

_____

_____

_____

_____

_____

_____

_____

_____

BECOMING JOURNAL

Do for yourself what you would freely give or do for another.

Date: _____

Time(s) or Repeating Numbers: _____

Songs: _____

Bible Passages/Books/Other Resources: _____

Animals/Birds: _____

Divination Tools/Crystals: _____

Thoughts/Feelings/Dreams: _____

_____

_____

_____

_____

_____

_____

_____

_____

_____

_____

_____

_____

_____

BECOMING JOURNAL

Open your heart to see infinite possibilities.

Date: _____

Time(s) or Repeating Numbers: _____

Songs: _____

Bible Passages/Books/Other Resources: _____

Animals/Birds: _____

Divination Tools/Crystals: _____

Thoughts/Feelings/Dreams: _____

_____

_____

_____

_____

_____

_____

_____

_____

_____

_____

_____

_____

BECOMING JOURNAL

Take time to go outside and spend time in nature.

Date: _____

Time(s) or Repeating Numbers: _____

Songs: _____

Bible Passages/Books/Other Resources: _____

Animals/Birds: _____

Divination Tools/Crystals: _____

Thoughts/Feelings/Dreams: _____

_____

_____

_____

_____

_____

_____

_____

_____

_____

_____

_____

_____

BECOMING JOURNAL

Love yourself enough to follow your dreams!

Date: _____

Time(s) or Repeating Numbers: _____

Songs: _____

Bible Passages/Books/Other Resources: _____

Animals/Birds: _____

Divination Tools/Crystals: _____

Thoughts/Feelings/Dreams: _____

_____

_____

_____

_____

_____

_____

_____

_____

_____

_____

_____

_____

BECOMING JOURNAL

Give yourself permission to heal by loving yourself unconditionally.

Date: _____

Time(s) or Repeating Numbers: _____

Songs: _____

Bible Passages/Books/Other Resources: _____

Animals/Birds: _____

Divination Tools/Crystals: _____

Thoughts/Feelings/Dreams: _____

_____

_____

_____

_____

_____

_____

_____

_____

_____

_____

_____

_____

BECOMING JOURNAL

Release the desire to ask for others' opinions. They will always respond from a place of what is best for them with regards to you.

Date: _____

Time(s) or Repeating Numbers: _____

Songs: _____

Bible Passages/Books/Other Resources: _____

Animals/Birds: _____

Divination Tools/Crystals: _____

Thoughts/Feelings/Dreams: _____

_____

_____

_____

_____

_____

_____

_____

_____

_____

_____

_____

_____

BECOMING JOURNAL

Stand up for your beliefs and let your power and integrity shine.

Date: _____

Time(s) or Repeating Numbers: _____

Songs: _____

Bible Passages/Books/Other Resources: _____

Animals/Birds: _____

Divination Tools/Crystals: _____

Thoughts/Feelings/Dreams: _____

_____

_____

_____

_____

_____

_____

_____

_____

_____

_____

_____

_____

_____

BECOMING JOURNAL

You are the light in this world.

*Do not let others dim your light which is the
eternal flame that exists within you.*

Date: _____

Time(s) or Repeating Numbers: _____

Songs: _____

Bible Passages/Books/Other Resources: _____

Animals/Birds: _____

Divination Tools/Crystals: _____

Thoughts/Feelings/Dreams: _____

_____

_____

_____

_____

_____

_____

_____

_____

_____

_____

BECOMING JOURNAL

Be bold.

Be brave.

Be confident as it is your birthright!

Date: _____

Time(s) or Repeating Numbers: _____

Songs: _____

Bible Passages/Books/Other Resources: _____

Animals/Birds: _____

Divination Tools/Crystals: _____

Thoughts/Feelings/Dreams: _____

_____

_____

_____

_____

_____

_____

_____

_____

_____

BECOMING JOURNAL

You are never alone. You are always surrounded
and loved by God and His messengers.

Date: _____

Time(s) or Repeating Numbers: _____

Songs: _____

Bible Passages/Books/Other Resources: _____

Animals/Birds: _____

Divination Tools/Crystals: _____

Thoughts/Feelings/Dreams: _____

_____

_____

_____

_____

_____

_____

_____

_____

_____

_____

_____

BECOMING JOURNAL

Mother Mary reminds us to trust in the Father.

He will never leave you.

Date: _____

Time(s) or Repeating Numbers: _____

Songs: _____

Bible Passages/Books/Other Resources: _____

Animals/Birds: _____

Divination Tools/Crystals: _____

Thoughts/Feelings/Dreams: _____

_____

_____

_____

_____

_____

_____

_____

_____

_____

_____

_____

BECOMING JOURNAL

*Do not shrink; do not become invisible or make yourself
small to make others feel comfortable.*

Date: _____

Time(s) or Repeating Numbers: _____

Songs: _____

Bible Passages/Books/Other Resources: _____

Animals/Birds: _____

Divination Tools/Crystals: _____

Thoughts/Feelings/Dreams:_____

_____

_____

_____

_____

_____

_____

_____

_____

_____

_____

_____

BECOMING JOURNAL

Forgive yourself and heal the past. God has already forgiven you. Release and let him carry your burdens.

Date: _____

Time(s) or Repeating Numbers: _____

Songs: _____

Bible Passages/Books/Other Resources: _____

Animals/Birds: _____

Divination Tools/Crystals: _____

Thoughts/Feelings/Dreams: _____

_____

_____

_____

_____

_____

_____

_____

_____

_____

_____

_____

_____

BECOMING JOURNAL

Know that every experience and relationship has been designed by the Universe to help you evolve and be the best person you can be. Recognize and affirm that you are exactly where you are supposed to be.

Date: _____

Time(s) or Repeating Numbers: _____

Songs: _____

Bible Passages/Books/Other Resources: _____

Animals/Birds: _____

Divination Tools/Crystals: _____

Thoughts/Feelings/Dreams: _____

_____

_____

_____

_____

_____

_____

_____

_____

_____

_____

_____

BECOMING JOURNAL

*Happily Ever After is available to you now and
in the future. You just have to believe.*

Date: _____

Time(s) or Repeating Numbers: _____

Songs: _____

Bible Passages/Books/Other Resources: _____

Animals/Birds: _____

Divination Tools/Crystals: _____

Thoughts/Feelings/Dreams: _____

_____

_____

_____

_____

_____

_____

_____

_____

_____

_____

_____

BECOMING JOURNAL

*Focus on your own healing and take responsibility
for your personal growth.*

Date: _____

Time(s) or Repeating Numbers: _____

Songs: _____

Bible Passages/Books/Other Resources: _____

Animals/Birds: _____

Divination Tools/Crystals: _____

Thoughts/Feelings/Dreams: _____

_____

_____

_____

_____

_____

_____

_____

_____

_____

_____

_____

_____

_____

BECOMING JOURNAL

Change and heal only the parts of you that YOU want to change.

Date: _____

Time(s) or Repeating Numbers: _____

Songs: _____

Bible Passages/Books/Other Resources: _____

Animals/Birds: _____

Divination Tools/Crystals: _____

Thoughts/Feelings/Dreams: _____

_____

_____

_____

_____

_____

_____

_____

_____

_____

_____

_____

BECOMING JOURNAL

You are free to be you!

Date: _____

Time(s) or Repeating Numbers: _____

Songs: _____

Bible Passages/Books/Other Resources: _____

Animals/Birds: _____

Divination Tools/Crystals: _____

Thoughts/Feelings/Dreams: _____

_____

_____

_____

_____

_____

_____

_____

_____

_____

_____

_____

BECOMING JOURNAL

What is it that you most want to do in life?

Date: _____

Time(s) or Repeating Numbers: _____

Songs: _____

Bible Passages/Books/Other Resources: _____

Animals/Birds: _____

Divination Tools/Crystals: _____

Thoughts/Feelings/Dreams: _____

_____

_____

_____

_____

_____

_____

_____

_____

_____

_____

_____

_____

BECOMING JOURNAL

Release the imprint of doing what other people think you "should" do. Follow your own path and do what brings you joy.

Date: _____

Time(s) or Repeating Numbers: _____

Songs: _____

Bible Passages/Books/Other Resources: _____

Animals/Birds: _____

Divination Tools/Crystals: _____

Thoughts/Feelings/Dreams: _____

_____

_____

_____

_____

_____

_____

_____

_____

_____

_____

_____

_____

BECOMING JOURNAL

The actions and reactions of others reveal their deepest shadows of fear.

Date: _____

Time(s) or Repeating Numbers: _____

Songs: _____

Bible Passages/Books/Other Resources: _____

Animals/Birds: _____

Divination Tools/Crystals: _____

Thoughts/Feelings/Dreams: _____

_____

_____

_____

_____

_____

_____

_____

_____

_____

_____

_____

_____

BECOMING JOURNAL

*Stay true to your essence of oneness with God. Continue
to give your fears and worries to the Creator.*

Date: _____

Time(s) or Repeating Numbers: _____

Songs: _____

Bible Passages/Books/Other Resources: _____

Animals/Birds: _____

Divination Tools/Crystals: _____

Thoughts/Feelings/Dreams: _____

_____

_____

_____

_____

_____

_____

_____

_____

_____

_____

_____

BECOMING JOURNAL

Your biggest opponent is your own inner critic.
Tell it to take a hike! You've got this!

Date: _____

Time(s) or Repeating Numbers: _____

Songs: _____

Bible Passages/Books/Other Resources: _____

Animals/Birds: _____

Divination Tools/Crystals: _____

Thoughts/Feelings/Dreams: _____

_____

_____

_____

_____

_____

_____

_____

_____

_____

_____

_____

_____

BECOMING JOURNAL

Make your decisions based on what brings you the most joy.

Date: _____

Time(s) or Repeating Numbers: _____

Songs: _____

Bible Passages/Books/Other Resources: _____

Animals/Birds: _____

Divination Tools/Crystals: _____

Thoughts/Feelings/Dreams: _____

_____

_____

_____

_____

_____

_____

_____

_____

_____

_____

_____

_____

BECOMING JOURNAL

Check to see if your fears are real or perceived. If perceived, that is your ego doing its best to keep you from claiming your power.

Date: _____

Time(s) or Repeating Numbers: _____

Songs: _____

Bible Passages/Books/Other Resources: _____

Animals/Birds: _____

Divination Tools/Crystals: _____

Thoughts/Feelings/Dreams: _____

_____

_____

_____

_____

_____

_____

_____

_____

_____

BECOMING JOURNAL

Take time to nurture yourself today.

Date: _____

Time(s) or Repeating Numbers: _____

Songs: _____

Bible Passages/Books/Other Resources: _____

Animals/Birds: _____

Divination Tools/Crystals: _____

Thoughts/Feelings/Dreams: _____

_____

_____

_____

_____

_____

_____

_____

_____

_____

_____

_____

_____

_____

BECOMING JOURNAL

Learn to set boundaries for yourself.

Date: _____

Time(s) or Repeating Numbers: _____

Songs: _____

Bible Passages/Books/Other Resources: _____

Animals/Birds: _____

Divination Tools/Crystals: _____

Thoughts/Feelings/Dreams: _____

_____

_____

_____

_____

_____

_____

_____

_____

_____

_____

_____

_____

_____

BECOMING JOURNAL

Have trust in yourself that all will be well.

And it will.

Date: _____

Time(s) or Repeating Numbers: _____

Songs: _____

Bible Passages/Books/Other Resources: _____

Animals/Birds: _____

Divination Tools/Crystals: _____

Thoughts/Feelings/Dreams: _____

_____

_____

_____

_____

_____

_____

_____

_____

_____

_____

_____

_____

BECOMING JOURNAL

*Ask God for help and reassurance. The Universe
will always respond if you ask.*

Date: _____

Time(s) or Repeating Numbers: _____

Songs: _____

Bible Passages/Books/Other Resources: _____

Animals/Birds: _____

Divination Tools/Crystals: _____

Thoughts/Feelings/Dreams: _____

_____

_____

_____

_____

_____

_____

_____

_____

_____

_____

_____

BECOMING JOURNAL

Be who you were meant to be-larger than life, powerful and confident.

Date: _____

Time(s) or Repeating Numbers: _____

Songs: _____

Bible Passages/Books/Other Resources: _____

Animals/Birds: _____

Divination Tools/Crystals: _____

Thoughts/Feelings/Dreams: _____

_____

_____

_____

_____

_____

_____

_____

_____

_____

_____

_____

_____

BECOMING JOURNAL

Breathe.

Everything is always in Divine and perfect order.

Date: _____

Time(s) or Repeating Numbers: _____

Songs: _____

Bible Passages/Books/Other Resources: _____

Animals/Birds: _____

Divination Tools/Crystals: _____

Thoughts/Feelings/Dreams: _____

_____

_____

_____

_____

_____

_____

_____

_____

_____

_____

_____

BECOMING JOURNAL

Sit outside and listen with your heart to the sounds of the Universe. Close your eyes and envision a world of love – for what you send out is what is returned to you.

Date: _____

Time(s) or Repeating Numbers: _____

Songs: _____

Bible Passages/Books/Other Resources: _____

Animals/Birds: _____

Divination Tools/Crystals: _____

Thoughts/Feelings/Dreams: _____

_____

_____

_____

_____

_____

_____

_____

_____

_____

_____

_____

_____

BECOMING JOURNAL

Be strong in faith and walk it with courage and conviction.

Date: _____

Time(s) or Repeating Numbers: _____

Songs: _____

Bible Passages/Books/Other Resources: _____

Animals/Birds: _____

Divination Tools/Crystals: _____

Thoughts/Feelings/Dreams: _____

_____

_____

_____

_____

_____

_____

_____

_____

_____

_____

_____

_____

BECOMING JOURNAL

Love others unconditionally and thank them
for the lessons that you learned.

Date: _____

Time(s) or Repeating Numbers: _____

Songs: _____

Bible Passages/Books/Other Resources: _____

Animals/Birds: _____

Divination Tools/Crystals: _____

Thoughts/Feelings/Dreams: _____

_____

_____

_____

_____

_____

_____

_____

_____

_____

_____

_____

_____

BECOMING JOURNAL

Love and cherish yourself unconditionally.

Date: _____

Time(s) or Repeating Numbers: _____

Songs: _____

Bible Passages/Books/Other Resources: _____

Animals/Birds: _____

Divination Tools/Crystals: _____

Thoughts/Feelings/Dreams: _____

_____

_____

_____

_____

_____

_____

_____

_____

_____

_____

_____

_____

BECOMING JOURNAL

Today is a blank page upon which you can choose to write your story.

Date: _____

Time(s) or Repeating Numbers: _____

Songs: _____

Bible Passages/Books/Other Resources: _____

Animals/Birds: _____

Divination Tools/Crystals: _____

Thoughts/Feelings/Dreams: _____

_____

_____

_____

_____

_____

_____

_____

_____

_____

_____

_____

_____

_____

BECOMING JOURNAL

Each moment is an opportunity to make a wish and change your course.

Date: _____

Time(s) or Repeating Numbers: _____

Songs: _____

Bible Passages/Books/Other Resources: _____

Animals/Birds: _____

Divination Tools/Crystals: _____

Thoughts/Feelings/Dreams: _____

_____

_____

_____

_____

_____

_____

_____

_____

_____

_____

_____

BECOMING JOURNAL

Before you go to bed at night, reflect upon:

Was I a reflection of love today?

Did I see love in others?

Did I love today with my whole heart?

Date: _____

Time(s) or Repeating Numbers: _____

Songs: _____

Bible Passages/Books/Other Resources: _____

Animals/Birds: _____

Divination Tools/Crystals: _____

Thoughts/Feelings/Dreams: _____

_____

_____

_____

_____

_____

_____

_____

_____

_____

BECOMING JOURNAL

No one is more powerful than you.

Date: _____

Time(s) or Repeating Numbers: _____

Songs: _____

Bible Passages/Books/Other Resources: _____

Animals/Birds: _____

Divination Tools/Crystals: _____

Thoughts/Feelings/Dreams: _____

_____

_____

_____

_____

_____

_____

_____

_____

_____

_____

_____

_____

BECOMING JOURNAL

*Trust that the changes you are experiencing are
for the best. Find the good in everything.*

Date: _____

Time(s) or Repeating Numbers: _____

Songs: _____

Bible Passages/Books/Other Resources: _____

Animals/Birds: _____

Divination Tools/Crystals: _____

Thoughts/Feelings/Dreams: _____

_____

_____

_____

_____

_____

_____

_____

_____

_____

_____

_____

BECOMING JOURNAL

You can do it. Take one step towards your goals today.

Date: _____

Time(s) or Repeating Numbers: _____

Songs: _____

Bible Passages/Books/Other Resources: _____

Animals/Birds: _____

Divination Tools/Crystals: _____

Thoughts/Feelings/Dreams: _____

_____

_____

_____

_____

_____

_____

_____

_____

_____

_____

_____

_____

_____

BECOMING JOURNAL

Take time to honor, heal and love your inner child.
What is it that he/she needs today?

Date: _____

Time(s) or Repeating Numbers: _____

Songs: _____

Bible Passages/Books/Other Resources: _____

Animals/Birds: _____

Divination Tools/Crystals: _____

Thoughts/Feelings/Dreams: _____

_____

_____

_____

_____

_____

_____

_____

_____

_____

_____

_____

BECOMING JOURNAL

Something wondrous and magical is about to happen.

BELIEVE!

Date: _____

Time(s) or Repeating Numbers: _____

Songs: _____

Bible Passages/Books/Other Resources: _____

Animals/Birds: _____

Divination Tools/Crystals: _____

Thoughts/Feelings/Dreams: _____

_____

_____

_____

_____

_____

_____

_____

_____

_____

_____

_____

_____

BECOMING JOURNAL

All that you feel is part of your transformation and necessary
for you to release that which has been holding you back.
Honor your emotions and let them flow freely.

Date: _____

Time(s) or Repeating Numbers: _____

Songs: _____

Bible Passages/Books/Other Resources: _____

Animals/Birds: _____

Divination Tools/Crystals: _____

Thoughts/Feelings/Dreams: _____

_____

_____

_____

_____

_____

_____

_____

_____

_____

_____

_____

BECOMING JOURNAL

*You are perfect just the way you are. There is nothing that
you need to change or fix. Let your inner beauty shine.*

Date: _____

Time(s) or Repeating Numbers: _____

Songs: _____

Bible Passages/Books/Other Resources: _____

Animals/Birds: _____

Divination Tools/Crystals: _____

Thoughts/Feelings/Dreams: _____

_____

_____

_____

_____

_____

_____

_____

_____

_____

_____

_____

BECOMING JOURNAL

Treat yourself with the same love you give to others. Be gentle and kind to yourself and see only love reflected in you.

Date: _____

Time(s) or Repeating Numbers: _____

Songs: _____

Bible Passages/Books/Other Resources: _____

Animals/Birds: _____

Divination Tools/Crystals: _____

Thoughts/Feelings/Dreams: _____

_____

_____

_____

_____

_____

_____

_____

_____

_____

_____

_____

BECOMING JOURNAL

You are loved.

You are worthy.

You are enough.

Date: _____

Time(s) or Repeating Numbers: _____

Songs: _____

Bible Passages/Books/Other Resources: _____

Animals/Birds: _____

Divination Tools/Crystals: _____

Thoughts/Feelings/Dreams: _____

_____

_____

_____

_____

_____

_____

_____

_____

_____

_____

BECOMING JOURNAL

Share your amazing self with the world!

Date: _____

Time(s) or Repeating Numbers: _____

Songs: _____

Bible Passages/Books/Other Resources: _____

Animals/Birds: _____

Divination Tools/Crystals: _____

Thoughts/Feelings/Dreams: _____

_____

_____

_____

_____

_____

_____

_____

_____

_____

_____

_____

_____

BECOMING JOURNAL

You are confident.

You are worthy.

You are strong and capable.

Date: _____

Time(s) or Repeating Numbers: _____

Songs: _____

Bible Passages/Books/Other Resources: _____

Animals/Birds: _____

Divination Tools/Crystals: _____

Thoughts/Feelings/Dreams: _____

_____

_____

_____

_____

_____

_____

_____

_____

_____

_____

BECOMING JOURNAL

Speak your truth always.

Date: _____

Time(s) or Repeating Numbers: _____

Songs: _____

Bible Passages/Books/Other Resources: _____

Animals/Birds: _____

Divination Tools/Crystals: _____

Thoughts/Feelings/Dreams: _____

_____

_____

_____

_____

_____

_____

_____

_____

_____

_____

_____

_____

BECOMING JOURNAL

Be your own best friend!

Date: _____

Time(s) or Repeating Numbers: _____

Songs: _____

Bible Passages/Books/Other Resources: _____

Animals/Birds: _____

Divination Tools/Crystals: _____

Thoughts/Feelings/Dreams: _____

_____

_____

_____

_____

_____

_____

_____

_____

_____

_____

_____

_____

BECOMING JOURNAL

*Visualize all the wonderful things, people and places
that you want to bring into your life.*

Date: _____

Time(s) or Repeating Numbers: _____

Songs: _____

Bible Passages/Books/Other Resources: _____

Animals/Birds: _____

Divination Tools/Crystals: _____

Thoughts/Feelings/Dreams: _____

_____

_____

_____

_____

_____

_____

_____

_____

_____

_____

_____

BECOMING JOURNAL

There is nothing for you to fear. Know that you are loved and protected and everything is always unfolding in Divine and perfect order.

Date: _____

Time(s) or Repeating Numbers: _____

Songs: _____

Bible Passages/Books/Other Resources: _____

Animals/Birds: _____

Divination Tools/Crystals: _____

Thoughts/Feelings/Dreams: _____

_____

_____

_____

_____

_____

_____

_____

_____

_____

_____

_____

_____

BECOMING JOURNAL

You have the power to change your course at any time. Set sail for your destination and enjoy the journey on the way to where you are going.

Date: _____

Time(s) or Repeating Numbers: _____

Songs: _____

Bible Passages/Books/Other Resources: _____

Animals/Birds: _____

Divination Tools/Crystals: _____

Thoughts/Feelings/Dreams: _____

_____

_____

_____

_____

_____

_____

_____

_____

_____

_____

_____

BECOMING JOURNAL

*The cost of not following your dreams could lead to depression,
anger and resentment. It's never too late to start! Start Now!!*

Date: _____

Time(s) or Repeating Numbers: _____

Songs: _____

Bible Passages/Books/Other Resources: _____

Animals/Birds: _____

Divination Tools/Crystals: _____

Thoughts/Feelings/Dreams: _____

_____

_____

_____

_____

_____

_____

_____

_____

_____

_____

_____

_____

BECOMING JOURNAL

Your purpose is to live life on your own terms. Do what you are passionate about and do no harm. Live your life with a sense of joy and satisfaction. Remove the word "obligation" from your vocabulary.

Date: _____

Time(s) or Repeating Numbers: _____

Songs: _____

Bible Passages/Books/Other Resources: _____

Animals/Birds: _____

Divination Tools/Crystals: _____

Thoughts/Feelings/Dreams: _____

_____

_____

_____

_____

_____

_____

_____

_____

_____

_____

_____

BECOMING JOURNAL

You are the only one holding you back. Take responsibility and break free of the past.

Date: _____

Time(s) or Repeating Numbers: _____

Songs: _____

Bible Passages/Books/Other Resources: _____

Animals/Birds: _____

Divination Tools/Crystals: _____

Thoughts/Feelings/Dreams: _____

_____

_____

_____

_____

_____

_____

_____

_____

_____

_____

_____

BECOMING JOURNAL

Life is eternal and everlasting and folds into itself –

Never lost and never the same.

Date: _____

Time(s) or Repeating Numbers: _____

Songs: _____

Bible Passages/Books/Other Resources: _____

Animals/Birds: _____

Divination Tools/Crystals: _____

Thoughts/Feelings/Dreams: _____

_____

_____

_____

_____

_____

_____

_____

_____

_____

_____

_____

BECOMING JOURNAL

*Every single living thing is always doing the best that
they know how to do and be in that moment.*

Date: _____

Time(s) or Repeating Numbers: _____

Songs: _____

Bible Passages/Books/Other Resources: _____

Animals/Birds: _____

Divination Tools/Crystals: _____

Thoughts/Feelings/Dreams: _____

_____

_____

_____

_____

_____

_____

_____

_____

_____

_____

BECOMING JOURNAL

Let your imagination and creativity flow – without judgment.

Date: _____

Time(s) or Repeating Numbers: _____

Songs: _____

Bible Passages/Books/Other Resources: _____

Animals/Birds: _____

Divination Tools/Crystals: _____

Thoughts/Feelings/Dreams: _____

_____

_____

_____

_____

_____

_____

_____

_____

_____

_____

_____

_____

_____

BECOMING JOURNAL

Your heart knows the way.

Listen.

Date: _____

Time(s) or Repeating Numbers: _____

Songs: _____

Bible Passages/Books/Other Resources: _____

Animals/Birds: _____

Divination Tools/Crystals: _____

Thoughts/Feelings/Dreams: _____

_____

_____

_____

_____

_____

_____

_____

_____

_____

_____

_____

_____

BECOMING JOURNAL

Accept and love yourself without judgment. It is the gift you give to yourself and others and it is the gift that God endowed to each of us.

Date: _____

Time(s) or Repeating Numbers: _____

Songs: _____

Bible Passages/Books/Other Resources: _____

Animals/Birds: _____

Divination Tools/Crystals: _____

Thoughts/Feelings/Dreams: _____

_____

_____

_____

_____

_____

_____

_____

_____

_____

_____

_____

_____

BECOMING JOURNAL

Connect with your breath!

Date: _____

Time(s) or Repeating Numbers: _____

Songs: _____

Bible Passages/Books/Other Resources: _____

Animals/Birds: _____

Divination Tools/Crystals: _____

Thoughts/Feelings/Dreams: _____

_____

_____

_____

_____

_____

_____

_____

_____

_____

_____

_____

_____

_____

BECOMING JOURNAL

Following Divine guidance is the key to opening up your intuition.

Date: _____

Time(s) or Repeating Numbers: _____

Songs: _____

Bible Passages/Books/Other Resources: _____

Animals/Birds: _____

Divination Tools/Crystals: _____

Thoughts/Feelings/Dreams: _____

_____

_____

_____

_____

_____

_____

_____

_____

_____

_____

_____

_____

BECOMING JOURNAL

*Belief and faith is believing in things that you cannot touch
or see and knowing that something greater exists.*

Date: _____

Time(s) or Repeating Numbers: _____

Songs: _____

Bible Passages/Books/Other Resources: _____

Animals/Birds: _____

Divination Tools/Crystals: _____

Thoughts/Feelings/Dreams: _____

_____

_____

_____

_____

_____

_____

_____

_____

_____

_____

_____

_____

BECOMING JOURNAL

Look below the surface to see the beauty and love in all things.

Date: _____

Time(s) or Repeating Numbers: _____

Songs: _____

Bible Passages/Books/Other Resources: _____

Animals/Birds: _____

Divination Tools/Crystals: _____

Thoughts/Feelings/Dreams: _____

_____

_____

_____

_____

_____

_____

_____

_____

_____

_____

_____

_____

BECOMING JOURNAL

Trust that God's plan for you is better than you could ever imagine!

Date: _____

Time(s) or Repeating Numbers: _____

Songs: _____

Bible Passages/Books/Other Resources: _____

Animals/Birds: _____

Divination Tools/Crystals: _____

Thoughts/Feelings/Dreams: _____

_____

_____

_____

_____

_____

_____

_____

_____

_____

_____

_____

_____

BECOMING JOURNAL

Suffering is optional. It's all in perspective.

Date: _____

Time(s) or Repeating Numbers: _____

Songs: _____

Bible Passages/Books/Other Resources: _____

Animals/Birds: _____

Divination Tools/Crystals: _____

Thoughts/Feelings/Dreams: _____

_____

_____

_____

_____

_____

_____

_____

_____

_____

_____

_____

_____

_____

BECOMING JOURNAL

Learn to sing your own song.

Date: _____

Time(s) or Repeating Numbers: _____

Songs: _____

Bible Passages/Books/Other Resources: _____

Animals/Birds: _____

Divination Tools/Crystals: _____

Thoughts/Feelings/Dreams: _____

_____

_____

_____

_____

_____

_____

_____

_____

_____

_____

_____

_____

BECOMING JOURNAL

Life is always about infinite possibilities!

Date: _____

Time(s) or Repeating Numbers: _____

Songs: _____

Bible Passages/Books/Other Resources: _____

Animals/Birds: _____

Divination Tools/Crystals: _____

Thoughts/Feelings/Dreams: _____

_____

_____

_____

_____

_____

_____

_____

_____

_____

_____

_____

_____

BECOMING JOURNAL

Being a good person is both passive and active.
We need to always choose what is right.

Date: _____

Time(s) or Repeating Numbers: _____

Songs: _____

Bible Passages/Books/Other Resources: _____

Animals/Birds: _____

Divination Tools/Crystals: _____

Thoughts/Feelings/Dreams: _____

_____

_____

_____

_____

_____

_____

_____

_____

_____

_____

_____

_____

BECOMING JOURNAL

Each of us is to inspire, help and guide others.

Date: _____

Time(s) or Repeating Numbers: _____

Songs: _____

Bible Passages/Books/Other Resources: _____

Animals/Birds: _____

Divination Tools/Crystals: _____

Thoughts/Feelings/Dreams: _____

_____

_____

_____

_____

_____

_____

_____

_____

_____

_____

_____

_____

BECOMING JOURNAL

Sometimes there is no answer to the "whys" in life. This is when we must surrender to the unknown and trust that all is in Divine and perfect order.

Date: _____

Time(s) or Repeating Numbers: _____

Songs: _____

Bible Passages/Books/Other Resources: _____

Animals/Birds: _____

Divination Tools/Crystals: _____

Thoughts/Feelings/Dreams: _____

_____

_____

_____

_____

_____

_____

_____

_____

_____

_____

_____

BECOMING JOURNAL

God sees you and loves you. You have much to share with the world. See yourself from a higher perspective.

Date: _____

Time(s) or Repeating Numbers: _____

Songs: _____

Bible Passages/Books/Other Resources: _____

Animals/Birds: _____

Divination Tools/Crystals: _____

Thoughts/Feelings/Dreams: _____

_____

_____

_____

_____

_____

_____

_____

_____

_____

_____

_____

BECOMING JOURNAL

*You have the power to heal yourself. Work with
and follow your inner guidance.*

Date: _____

Time(s) or Repeating Numbers: _____

Songs: _____

Bible Passages/Books/Other Resources: _____

Animals/Birds: _____

Divination Tools/Crystals: _____

Thoughts/Feelings/Dreams: _____

_____

_____

_____

_____

_____

_____

_____

_____

_____

_____

_____

BECOMING JOURNAL

When you find yourself out on a limb, trust that you can fly!

Date: _____

Time(s) or Repeating Numbers: _____

Songs: _____

Bible Passages/Books/Other Resources: _____

Animals/Birds: _____

Divination Tools/Crystals: _____

Thoughts/Feelings/Dreams: _____

_____

_____

_____

_____

_____

_____

_____

_____

_____

_____

_____

_____

Printed in the United States
By Bookmasters